C000100850

THE DIAMOND SOUL

Andrew D Harry RPP PTP

www.becoming.me.uk

© Andrew D Harry RPP PTP 2018, 2019 & 2020, unless otherwise stated herein. The moral right of the author has been asserted according to the Copyright, Designs and Patents Act 1988.

All rights reserved. No part of this publication may be reproduced, stored in a retrieval system or transmitted, in any form or by any means, electronic, mechanical, photocopying, recording or otherwise, without the prior permission of the author. This book is sold subject to the condition that it shall not, by way of trade or otherwise, be lent, resold, hired out or otherwise circulated without the author's prior consent in any form of binding or cover other than that in which it is published and without a similar condition including this condition being imposed on the subsequent purchaser. A catalogue card for this book is available from the British Library.

Paperback ISBN: 978-1-8380345-0-4

eBook ISBN: 978-1-8380345-1-1

This book has not been created to be specific to any individual's or organizations' situation or needs. Every effort has been made to make this book as accurate as possible. This book should serve only as a general guide and not as the ultimate source of subject information. This book contains information that might be dated and is intended only to educate and entertain. The author shall have no liability or responsibility to any person or entity regarding any loss or damage incurred, or alleged to have incurred, directly or indirectly, by the information contained in this book.

DEDICATION

To my children, Samuel, Alice and Robyn, to
my wife Joy, our extended family and all my
friends worldwide.

Thank you all for your love and support.

CONTENTS

Acknowledgments i
Author's Note v
Introduction 1
1. Unalome 3
2. Winter Sun 5
3. Incessant Fear 6
4. Eat Drink Work Sleep 8
5. Arrogance 9
6. Breaking the Spell 11
7. Out of Reach 13
8. Fractured Narrative 15
9. Vitality 17
10. Another Tune 18
11. Delightfully Wrong 21
12. The Veil 24
13. Claim Your Peace 25
14. Identity 26
15. Blessed 29
16. Free-Fall 30
17. Cosmic Seed 32
18. Beyond Belief 34
19. Clarion Call 36
20. Le Carrelier 38
21. Mountain of Light 39
22. Becoming 44
23. Enceladus 46
24. Contentment 47
25. Gateway 49

26. Crossing the Rubicon 51

27. Out of the Blue.................................... 53

28. Sheltered Path 55

29. Mindful Meditation.............................. 56

30. Alignment 58

31. Superman 60

32. Sacred Lover...................................... 61

33. Courage 62

34. Paradox.. 63

35. New Light 64

36. Chocolate 65

37. Welcome 66

38. Faith 67

Epilogue.. 69

References and Notes................................. 70

About The Author..................................... 75

ACKNOWLEDGMENTS

Brian Nash, screen writer and passionate creator, thank you for the day. Graham & Lyn Whiteman, co-creators of The Relaxation Academy®. Peggy Goldreich, for your editorial panache. Rick Venning & Christine Rose for your wise counsel.

It's like we have spent our lives living in a darkened room, perilously clinging on to the ceiling, when we find that all we need do is let go. We fall onto a deep, soft, warm bed, the curtains are open, light floods in and we are greeted by a beautiful dawn chorus, as if for the first time.

Author's Note

This book is part autobiography and part technical manual. As a meditation aid it provides a radical and practical perspective for the reader to contemplate their relationship with mind, body, spirit and the natural world, to effectively breach the experienced status quo. It is aimed at nurturing a very grounded, personal enquiry into a more inclusive and accessible cosmology and a more holistic, connected and resourceful view of life. It invites the reader to explore a revolutionary and accessible discipline to seed active, personal rebellion. Encouraging, one soul at a time, I hope it can play its part in a global transformation.

Introduction

This book is a call to liberation and a medication-free trigger for change. It is a guide that investigates the nature of happiness and our intimate relationship to it. In two parts it examines the impact of everyone's initial quest outward and, for some, the subsequent journey back in. It is a distillation of the lessons I have learned over many years, overcoming chronic illness and as an experienced practitioner of energy medicine. This is my journey. In capturing it I invite the reader to tread a path of deep and powerful reconnection. As a salve to an over-burdened nervous system it can directly support health maintenance and recovery. This collection explores a way to end reliance on constructed patterns of a controlling, rigid, inner narrative and provides a safe and effective intervention to create beneficial change. I sincerely hope all will enjoy this little book and benefit from it as intended. So, relax deeply, feel better and enjoy your life more.

1. Unalome

The poets and sages of old, belovedly sold, the notion that there exists a plausible connection, a way to the light, where after suitable progress, through appropriate introspection, we will have become heaven blessed and our mere temporal lives will have ended. We will have transcended our baser nature and become physically, emotionally and spiritually wise and have realised that the ultimate prize lies at the end of our very own path to paradise. A rare few have attempted to share a path to this state of priceless detachment. Yet still, for many, suffering and pain remain sustained by the blight of attachment. The purpose of the telling is the response it elicits. If attempts fail then the teller, some might say, rests complicit in the great deception and can only claim success if the way is accessible without exception. Our understanding and experience share common ground. In both thinking and feeling life's content is found, although happiness will continue to be a fanciful illusion until a return to the primacy of feeling is our conclusion. If we operate in an identity that remains arrested in narcissistic deceit, we will never be truly free. So, unfasten reliance on this notion immediately. What is offered in this book is an invitation to look at the precise mechanism behind the journey to transcend the mechanical monkey mind and help you to find what it is you want. It is not the font of all knowledge that is true, but it will go some way to reveal exactly what is stopping you.[1]

---

[1] One of the two NLP Magic questions. Espoused in The Way of NLP by Joseph O'Connor and Ian McDermott, published by Thorsons, 2001.

2. Winter Sun

Winter sun slants off the water into my eyes. Seagull cries overhead. I sit on this bench alone, miles from home, knowing I could be with you instead. Here on my own, enslaved to the man, feeling like an also-ran in the great scheme of life. There must be more than this strife. Day in and day out I doubt they would hear me shout, even at the top of voice, but who are they to me? We shall see. Moving on then to more of the same, day in, day out, again and again. There must be more than this! No way out. They wouldn't even hear me shout. I don't even know what I'd have to say. Oh well, here's to the end of another day. I guess this is just how it is, but I can't help thinking, that there must be more to it all than this?

3. Incessant Fear

Disconnected. Out of reach. The beauty that I see, would still go on if I were gone, it's just that it wouldn't be seen by me. Life goes on relentlessly year on year. More life to be ended. I am worn out by an incessant fear, so harsh. If all there is to this is blood and sweat and worms, it is hardly a heart-warming thought, should it be for nought? All this toil and effort, what's it for? Going back to the earth to sustain more? More of the same uncaring life. If I am good, in a way they have defined, I will have achieved a life refined, but if the refinement of all this loss is a loss, I can't find a crumb of hope in it, just dross. Toil and effort to carve out this life. Perpetual moil, until I merge with the soil, to spread me even thinner. Even the worms that feast on me will be eaten by birds and the birds in turn will end up as something else's dinner. Instead of dreams of more grind, my goal is to rise above this, to find a place to soothe my soul. Whatever that is? Perhaps, away from this life, so unkind? Why would I put myself through more of the same, again and again? Through cycles of gloom, impending, never ending, doom. I might as well be kind to myself at least and end it all. Not in the vain hope of achieving some peace, but to be released and no longer suffer this shit. I wouldn't know then if it were to carry on without me, but the pain and my loss and this shit, would be gone.

4. Eat Drink Work Sleep

I am going to do something about this! I am fed up with this lonely, daily grind. In order to put my plan together I will need to find some time, but I haven't even got the time to think, just eat and drink and work and sleep. I am beginning to act like a sheep. Baa baa. Blah blah. Yes sir. No sir. Three bags full sir. Back in the groove, not able to move. Whirr, fizz, bleep. The machine goes on and on and on. Slowly, suddenly, all notions of hope are gone. Gone. Back in the groove, not able to move. Whirr, fizz, bleep. Eat, drink, work, sleep. My own ideas in full retreat. Whirr, fizz, bleep. Eat, drink, work, sleep. Whirr, fizz, bleep. Eat, drink, work, sleep.

5. Arrogance

Is it arrogance sublime, that I have given so much time and attention to automatic reactions, unwanted distractions, now beyond their prime? In giving credence to those thoughts unseen, I have allowed my fears to rule the roost, unchallenged, unfettered, my faults assumed, dominating. I have been paralysed, consumed. What possible, credible purpose is being served, in behaving like I do? If only I knew how to change the script. Just what can I do to help myself climb out of this self-imposed crypt and leave this zoo? I am slowly, cautiously, painfully, becoming aware of this log in my eye that so limits my view. If only I knew how to move it aside, I would no longer have to hide behind automatic responses designed to protect, but now only resulting in neglect of those I love and who love me too. I have just got to get out of this zoo. Piece by piece I will unravel this web, that so grieves my heart and confounds my head. I have decided that the only thing left to do right now is to work out how to start. I haven't a clue what to do, nor even how to begin. After all, what do I know, mere mortal that I am? As I sit here in this wretched state, wanting to know love, anticipating only hate. I am pathetic, wretched, all alone, racked with more of the same pain and shame. My only friend is my deep, unavoidable, cleansing grief, which has not yet offered even a crumb of relief. All my hope is gone. What to do, to get out of this zoo? I wish I knew.

6. Breaking the Spell

Turned down a different road today, on my way to lunch. Everything seemed so clear. My head was full of new ideas. I even acted on a hunch. I was fitful over the meeting at two and was frightened at what I thought others might do. Then over a tasty chicken soup, I stepped beyond my usual loop, of habitual reactions and emotional distractions, and realised it was my thoughts of what others might do that were tying me in knots. So frightened of my own projections, of fears, of habitually anticipated, future rejections. Now it is time to stop associating certainty with fear and instead begin to doubt the fear itself, when it sticks its head out. I choose to be certain instead, certain of something, of anything else, but not, for once, the commanding, demanding, ever expanding, fears in my head. I have been so overwhelmed, by this dominance of fear, that it has begun to become abundantly clear that what I think I hear, this sound of the pounding of dread, is not really real at all, it's all in my head. So, at long last I am going to choose to break the spell I have cast and choose to be certain instead. Certain? Certain of what? Well, certain of anything, but that fear in my head.

7. Out of Reach

Change is inevitable, perplexing. Vexing. Change? Without it I would remain the same, in misery, my soul failing. Failing in this wretched state, that I am beginning to hate. Round and round. Wretched loss prevailing. Fears, anxieties assailing. Everyone else tells me what to do, to think and do and be. They tell me how I must act in order to succeed. To be successful in this life is so fruitless, a chore. Why, would I want to succeed more, at satisfying a hidden man's need, just because he or she can shout and drown everyone else out? Telling me what to think, to eat, to drink, to love and hate. How did I get in this awful state? This state where I do as the hidden man pleases. "Do as 'he says' and you will be fine. You will have what you want and be free of diseases." To work some more and ruin my health? At least I will be on the road to wealth! Lining someone else's pockets, while surviving, when I could be thriving, a-living. Sitting here writing and reflecting upon this dross, all I can feel is a sense of loss. Which doesn't tie in with what I have been told. "Work hard, do as 'we say' and the streets will be paved with gold." Spend all my time focussing on someone else's definition of success and I will have all that I want? Instead, I get less! If what I want is defined by someone else, with changing needs, why should I bother? As soon as I reach the next level there's another and another. Another door, that wasn't apparent before. Still, a few more strides and I'll be there. At a place that is always being redefined, that routinely perplexes my mind and always remains just out of reach.

8. Fractured Narrative

Forget what the man says! What is it I really want? Well, since I was young it has been on the tip of my tongue, but I still don't know where to start. I've hardly even given it a moment's thought, as the man has had all my attention, my effort, my sinews, my heart. I suppose what I really want, is to know what is it I need. That's a beginning, a seed. If ever so tenuous, but why not? Everything else is becoming so bloody strenuous. I need to sleep-in and rest, get things off my chest, take some time to define, what is important to me and what it is I believe. What have I learned from this so far? Well, I have listened to everyone else for a start! From now on, I think I will take heed of myself and my heart. There is night and day, black and white, up and down, dark and light. I wake and sleep, may live and die.

There is in and out, below and above. There is beginning and end. Loss and gain. Hate and love. Different and the same. There is hot and cold. Having an opinion and being told. There is empty and full. There is high and low. There is hard and soft, and Sun and Moon, future and past, too late and too soon. It seems to me that in the world that I can see, there are always two sides to each story and the prevailing view presents only one side as the road to glory? If the man says this is right, it's surely quite possible that what he says is shite? It is, after all, only one part of the picture. At this juncture, I will certainly have to explore this a little more. As, even to dwell on the neutral space between risks conjuring a notion of extremes. An energising bridge, for sure, though it would be wise to be wary of being snared in a concept of opposites that, by definition, and without care, may sustain the fragility of these mindful conditions. Nonetheless, to meet[2] in this field would, indeed, be very neat.

---

[2] "Out beyond the ideas of right doing and wrong doing, there is a field. I will meet you there" – Rūmī.

9. Vitality

You may not know, but for life to exist at all, energy must flow[3] and a balanced state persist. According to universally accepted norms, energy is never lost, it merely changes form. Through observation, we have learned that positive potential converts to negative through a neutral field and then returns. North to south and back again, it's all very neat. The cycle occurs and the circuit is complete. If this harmony remains the cycle will repeat again and again, perpetually. Any departure from this state will cause the energy to dissipate and the health of the system to deteriorate. Recovering this crucial ambivalence ensures equity is once again obtained and vitality retained.

---

[3] The renowned "Flow Sequence" developed by Graham and Lyn Whiteman and as described in their book Stress Less, More Success, published by 10-10-10, 2015.

10. Another Tune

Well, well, what a day. What is this I say? "I couldn't possibly, definitely not!" but yes, these chains are released and out they trot. What to do with them when they reveal the opportunity to heal? I can choose to take hold of them and turn them round. Initially this sounds clumsy, out of sync, yet, each time I notice I can stop and drink them in until they begin to sing another tune. I can follow each thread wherever it leads, to new expressions, unseen needs. Gradually I can begin to feel the opposite of each could be just as real. What then, I ask, as I start to flow, what do I want? Only I can know. Only I can know, what I want to say or do, to act[4] and express

---

[4] Inspired by the book Life is Tremendous by Charles "Tremendous" Jones, wherein "whatever you believe, act as if it is true" challenges each of us to wrestle

myself, as I take a step along a brave new road. I can cast aside ideals imposed by others I have held in positions of misplaced authority. They cannot feel what I can feel[5], nor know what it is I need. I can trust myself! I am unique and the universe relies on the dreams I seed. I can seed those dreams and nurture them well and release myself from the bonds that hold. I have no need to doubt, but can choose to be certain, to be bold. I need merely hold my attention on what I choose. What it is I want to feel and choose to feel it again and again, as my doubts retreat. Slowly and inexorably I sense what it is to be certain. I can after all discern what it is I need, I have, I want, I feel, I am. Each time I take stock and know, that even though each seems a tiny step towards a distant star, in no time at all, the mighty bounds they have become reveal that I have travelled far. To

---

with the nature of belief.

[5] Here I relate to the monumental publication that is A Course in Miracles, by Helen Schucman, published in 1976. A year-long study of daily affirmations. A challenging and transformative read.

the growing edge[6] of the universe and back, to share what I have learned. To coax, cajole another soul, to know they won't get burned. When they leave the surface of their moon and plunge into the depths of their sun.

---

[6] Doctor Randolph Stone, the founder of Polarity Therapy used this term "the growing edge" to define our journey to challenge and push back our boundary conditions. Set out in two volumes, The Complete Collected Works by CLCS Wellness Books, Dr Stone's system is a vast treatise on the ancient modality of Energy Medicine. See www.ukpta.org.uk

11. Delightfully Wrong

I want to change the way I feel. Now, not in some hazy, distant moment, but I have always thought that I don't know how. Is somebody else somehow responsible for this, or is the solution waiting, hidden within me? What if I stopped going out and instead went more fully in? Will the echoes of my wounds still chill my soul, or could they quietly, gently start to sing another tune? Some help, as my efforts converge, assists the free flow of energy, provides a breakthrough, brings clarity. Connections appear, obviously. Is this an ancient opportunity? Am I free, to simply create a choice, to find the courage to know what is my truth and end my dependence on another's view? With compassion, I now choose to tread my own path, after what has seemed such a long time residing under the yoke of another man's dreams? It seems that I am beginning to believe that I am ready, to choose to exercise my power, through action and expression in each moment. In repeating this process, I have begun to begin to recognise my true nature and see that now in others too. Have I found a promising way out of this zoo?

In knowing what it is I want, I am beginning to be transformed and able to choose to transform more. In an endless cycle, revolving, involving, evolving, becoming grounded and certain. It is my right. Quickly and effortlessly, I surprise myself in my ability to be more fully me. As if for the first time a concept of safety begins to appear. Yet, it becomes clear, it has been and is always here and now, above and below, within and without. There is no need to further suffer any lingering trace of doubt. As I start to take my first, final, faltering steps along the road to becoming whole, I need not now assume that the road is arduous and long, but can entertain the thought that I might just be delightfully wrong. With patience and attention my rigid, inner shadows start to move. I am manifesting wholeness through the embodiment of love. First ascending, then descending, I know that love is here to stay. It cannot go away. Though fleeting, it is kindled and remains eternal. I embrace it. I know there is no need to chase it. For it is impatiently chasing me.

12. The Veil

Awareness may be seen as the screen[7] on which all my thoughts and ideas are projected? So, what is the source of this screen, that so intimately observes all the facets of my life, yet sits there for so long, undetected? Instead of waiting lifetimes then to discover what lies beyond the sand, the sea and sky, I can surely first try to seek to find this screen that lies unseen behind the unfathomable labyrinth of my mind. It seems to me that this obscure horizon could be the very source of my being. Now, that would certainly be exceedingly freeing, if true!

---

[7] The Hindu concept of jnana yoga, vichara (self-enquiry) as explored in David Godman's book Be As You Are, published by Penguin; reissue edition March 7, 1991.

13. Claim Your Peace

In your whole life have you ever known a moment without fear? Well, draw near, for I have a tale to tell. It may well come as some surprise that the mechanical mind cannot reprise the solution, but will certainly continue to deliver ever more light pollution. Let it do its job. It is not here to rob your soul, but to help you achieve your earth-bound goal. There is, however, no point waiting for the conflict to cease, to win this war you must first claim your peace.[8]

---

[8] Inspired by a conversation in an episode in series one of Star Trek Discovery, a Netflix Original Series, 2017.

14. Identity

Enough of this. I know there is more, know it at my very core. What it is I want to find, lies beyond the fractured screen of my mind. It is the certain ground of being that lies beyond the dimmed and intoxicating veil of my seeing. I choose now to change the way I deal with my life, again. I realise, that rabid corporations and ambitious men relentlessly and ruthlessly exploit the very nature of my mind to polarise. Carelessly wielding the sceptre of stolen, sovereign power, their misguided manipulation and my over-reliance on thought, have effectively wrought the equivalence of nought, vicariously. With breath-taking temerity in deploying such fake sincerity, they are hell-bent on destroying our culture and now fragile society. This phantom of phenomena so distracts and conceals and forges a tempting, endless path to my mind, so supposedly real. Relentless, in its drive, in pursuit of the prize. The germ of consent, generated, damns all to karmic servitude. This will persist, until we get real, resist and step off the peddled wheel of avarice and greed and take heed of what another might need. To renew this broken frame and reclaim our sovereignty, we need only remember once again, consciously, how to feel. Let me be clear, there is neither nostalgia nor effort here. In feeling, I can simply find my way and make a fresh new certain start. In every moment of every day, a tinge of certainty begins to hold sway. It is now assuredly and abundantly clear to me that I can only truly know what it is to be real, when I feel it in the neglected chambers of my heart. The exhaustive, effort of retreating to the veil behind my vulnerable mind can now be left behind, as it laboriously continues its computational task. A conceptual simulation? A clever algorithm, designed to compare and contrast, on its arduous, unending, ultimately disappointing[9] solitary and limiting quest? Just-in-time, this illusory identity, this great deception, this awareness of awareness, the Emperor's new self, can be returned, ready-for-use at a moment's notice, onto the tool shed's shelf. As I embark on a journey, so potent and profound, in a state of clarence,[10] to conjure a feeling, akin to the warmth from a curled up, drowsy kitten, nestled comfortable and safe, purring upon on my breast. Wherein, my simmering, true potential, my very soul, can quietly be found, beyond the maelstrom of my mind, where it has lain patiently waiting, deep within the comfort of my chest.

---

[9] Inspired by the book Krishnamurti and the Unity of Man by Carlo Suares, published in 1982 by Chetana, wherein Krishnamurti describes the moment when we become finally and fully disappointed by the mind.

[10] The affectionate name for a horse-drawn carriage with a clear glass front. Also, a term used to define the heir apparent within the British Monarchy. Here re-framed as the vehicle for radical reclamation of our sovereignty, a state in which we see the road ahead clearly, concurrent with experiencing the journey, safely and in comfort.

15. Blessed

My well-practiced need to control, born of anxiety and fear, has led me to here. Where even now I often try harder to control what I see or what I think is happening to me. I have unintentionally gone to some extraordinary lengths that test my strengths. Enduring physical, emotional and spiritual pain, without a jot of detectable gain. This clever cul-de-sac has served as an existential trap. Yet now in this more intimate place the less I try to seize control the more certain I become. The closer I am to home. I am blessed.

16. Free-Fall

Despite the mind's capacity to contrast and distract my attention can now settle on a centre, of unequalled precision. Where a certainty of self resides and replaces the mind's disappointing, peripheral, though nonetheless useful, vision. As if emerging from a mystical haze, I am now shielded from the Medusa's gaze. With ease embedded, I know with conviction, exactly, where my attention is headed. I am free to move through a lens of deepening love.

As silk flows over steel, there is no need to resist, but to simply feel my rested best.[11] I know what it is now to truly, be real, to exist. As I feel it, I can then choose to feel it, even more. Slowly, deftly, subtly, I approach a deeper, different, though essentially, familiar

---

[11] www.restedbest.co.uk.

shore. Ceasing to struggle, I float to a sacred isle and tarry on solid, certain ground a while. Transformed, the once vaguely sensed, dozing feline stirs from its mythical slumber, unfurling a muted though leonine-like roar. As I choose to feel it, I can choose to feel it even more. Ever deeper, fractally, repeatedly, to my very core. Then every day, in every way, I am a mere choice of letting go away. I now relish the opportunity to learn to relax more deeply, until once again I reach that content-free point where heart and soul are understood, for good. Without constraint, I free-fall within and then I free-fall some more. Into it again, I am certain and then I am certain, for sure. Each time more focussed, yet less intense. Each time I lose myself I find myself more. Each time as I feel there is less pretence. Each time refining in crystalline surety. Each time less alone and more at home. Like a life re-born. A new beginning, with each cycle, I know I am winning the race to the centre, to my rested-best, my very self. At this centre and at the growing edge of all, I stand a part, consciously grounded in my heart.

17. Cosmic Seed

My mind, wide-awake and aware of itself, is left reeling, I have realised that I cannot think this feeling.[12] A feeling of such depth and scope, that lies beyond the mindful dichotomy of fear and hope and the utility of effort and strife. It opens me to the whole where I find resides my soul, the very purpose of my life. So, relax and know that you too can recreate the conditions to make a simple choice, to either think or feel. A simple, yet apparently difficult decision, to truly, enduringly, certainly be real. No volition. No conditions. No opinions. No grievance. No difference. No preference. No hope. No fear. No now. No here. So, relax, feel better and enjoy life more. Refresh

---

[12] Trademark re-printed here with kind permission of www.heartenterprises.co.uk.

yourself. Drink it in. It is easier than you think. In this conscious awareness find the order that leads to the source of your essence, the cosmic seed.

18. Beyond Belief

My mind wide-awake and aware of itself is still reeling, in the realisation that consciousness is best accessed, not through perceptive thought, but from a simple feeling. For all my life it seemed to me, that the world is merely defined sensorily. I have assumed that these sensory filters deliver all that there is to think and sense and see. In believing thus, like a little wooden boy who within himself, devoid of any sense of joy, an empty shell, has programmed, woven even, his own limiting, personal spell, and alone has created a unique kind of hell. I have meticulously refined my own magic potion, to suffer and to ensure that I have remained a mere isolated drop in this vast ocean. Frightened, out of balance and at times unsettled, I still often try so hard to find what

I think will bring me peace of mind. The more I try to identify with all I sense and think and see the more I fall apart. I only now ever get it together when I simply remember to feel deeply within my heart. I have tried and tried to think myself out of this place, but with ever greater effort, the available space in my head gets less and less and I must confess that the problem is only ever solved when I give up my need to control and accept that all I need do is to feel, to let go. I am also moved to say that it has come as some relief to find a simple way to move beyond balance and belief, for the deeper I go, the more I feel, how far I reach. To open myself to the exposure, of confidence and composure, as I aspire to dwell in a certain centre that has its own deft pull, guaranteeing a feeling that is peaceable, calm and full. Like comfrey is nourished from the earth, radically, grow deeper into your certainty and know your worth. Trying to think this feeling is an impossible task. It is simply madness, so please don't ask.

19. Clarion Call

I have stumbled upon the answer to a question I did not think to ask. I had unwittingly unmasked, a folly of epic proportions, even now sustaining limiting, mindful, projections and distortions, that obscure a powerful truth. In learning to let go, we can describe consciousness and awareness as two distinct things, according to this kinaesthetic sleuth. The latter, you will find sustains a perpetual toil in your mind. The former, a feeling where the sky has no ceiling,[13] where mere ideas of love form but pale imitations to the ease found through simple relaxation. Know this and you and your soul will never again be seemingly

---

[13] Central to "The Esencia Model" presented at www.esencia.org.uk and beautifully articulated in the song "Audition (The Fools Who Dream)", from the Original Motion Picture Soundtrack of La La Land 2016.

parted. You will have become lionhearted.[14] So, let an inner, heartfelt roar well-up and send a clarion call far and wide, to invite one and all to join the pride.

---

[14] The Consequences of Relaxation as defined at www.lionhearted.org.uk.

20. Le Carrelier

The sun-baked soil reflects a portion of its heat onto my warming skin. My eyes squinting limit the intense light of day. Buzzing and swishing, sounds of wings, deftly fill my ears, as the air rises and rushes around me in its playful dance. No matter how intensely I strain my eyes to see, the fragrance of the blossom eludes me. Without volition on my part, the vital oils burst into scent. The heady note created completes its unlikely journey, momentarily, imparting its joy.

21. Mountain of Light

Approaching the summit, through a path hewn from rock, lies the Heaven's Gate. Where is found a majestic hall with polished black and white marble floors and intricately carved columnar walls. High above, a crystal ceiling clear to see, supported by an exquisitely forged and gilded frame, looks out onto a blazing night sky. Here, mesmerised by the grandeur of the space, it is disappointing that I can look out on this vast beyond, yet it will not yield to my touch. Time barred I can see, that to reach my home in the stars, I need find another way not previously evident to me. A more personal and complete cosmology? This glorious, yet vacuous and impersonal palace, now devoid of anything but temporal value, eludes to an implied purpose, a treasure, a chalice? I seek the barely sensible in the chill, wintry gloom. Ahead, steps ascend to an altar-like platform. I spy a shadowy gap, some way off to my right. How far? It's difficult to measure. Clutching at straws, I set off, intrigued. Imagination fuelling anticipation. Closer now, but not much clearer a cleft emerges as I edge nearer. Before me grey still forms. Impressions only, nothing certain. Slowly, gingerly pressing forward. My open hands reach out before me. Fingertips touch. A shiver spreads. I recoil. Velvet? Heavy, dense, beautiful fabric. Curtains of red! Parting them reveals nothing, but cool scent from spring flowers, carried on a zephyr beckoning me from below. Instinctively, I reckon, I should follow.

Taking one cautious step, reverentially, repeatedly I proceed. I feel my way in the dark. Tight steps rotating down, just my size. A helical staircase is revealed, descending clockwise. Carefully, trusting this hidden master's craft and without a backward glance, I disappear into this obsidian shaft. Dazzling darkness and deafening silence, tempered by the delightful breeze, accompany my slow, steady progress down and around. Reassured by the rhythm of my breath and my feet, my initially, impetuous belief is persuaded into faithful adherence, with the renewed promise of each reliable stride.

How far now? Not sure, but there is surely more? One step and then another. Just what will I discover? Or what might I miss, as I spiral further down into this abyss? Inevitably, the pace is slow as step by step I go. Steady and sure. Cautious and attentive. I find that I develop more trust in this process, though visually compromised. Foot falling echoes resound, reverberating, changing each time around. Progress? Not sure if there is more. Patience tested, senses rested, coiling deeper still. This darkness, now familiar, becomes comforting, real. I start to relish the reliance on something else and notice a shift in how I feel. Each turn repeats giving way to yet another. Further down and around relying only on breath and touch and sound. Without the filter of my eyes I start to sense things differently, through a new type of light. I stay in this feeling, persisting, though now growing agitated, disturbed. Fearful thoughts seep through to my mind, erratic and perturbed. Not yet panic, but close I know. Anxious. A tiger's tail, tentatively held. I stay with it and continue now, warily, down and around. Stay with it, now. Stay with it. Down and around. Down and around. Stay with it. Down and around. My fretful frenzy at its peak, resigned, I release the long, imaginary, caudal form. Directly, my descent stops, replaced by welcomed and solid ground. I settle to sit, silent and still, upon warm, dry, firm earth. Resting, catching my breath. I sit and rest some more. Eventually and unexpectedly there settles on me a sharper, gentler, more refined, delightful and certain, sense of self-worth. Perceptibly, my life-purpose instantly clear to me, the heavens above intimately near to me and each element intrinsically part of me. Firmly centred in this safe harbour, free from the need of more labour, intense, easy focus, contentment. In union now. I rise and walk with such ease, confidently and calmly. Without a care I return outside to sing to my trees, embracing and inhaling the fresh, evening air. Surprised by certainty. Like a day lent from summer, when the song sings itself.[15] Nothing is lost, everything regained. I carry within me a new-found clarity, framed in feeling, assuring me that this very personal sanctuary is always directly, accessible to me and directly, accessible to one and all.

---

[15] Poem of William Carlos Williams, American Poet, 1883-1963.

22. Becoming

Along the road to becoming whole, lies the building of the diamond soul. Mist hangs thick and cool. As the sun's rays elicit warmth for the new day. Rivulets of myth and bliss flow along the growing edge of the new dawn. Rose and lily, on window-ledge, scent the air.

Light streams on dreams and industry there. A knowing smile breaks out on all who enter the establishment of presence. It is a place to ground and truly connect to this hectic world of black and white and the illusion of wrong or right. To fuse with love another way and balance impulse gone astray, to clear the path to harmony. What I need is what I feel, it is what I want and have. I am the link to parity and a simple law of love. Now is the time to be myself and to move with clarity. To build upon foundations tested by gracious hearts and loving hands, I have rested. No longer whether, but instead when, without as within, the time is nigh. My feet touch the earth and my head the sky. I am in my element. Home at last, now I am able, to express and to involve, to bustle and hustle and take my place to nourish from my table. Without compromise or dilution, I will act on my own terms. I'll take no truck and pass no buck for there is work to do. Until subject and object are one, when the race will have been run, up the mountain of the Moon, on our journey to the Sun. My place can be found in the building of the diamond soul, that lies along the road to becoming whole.

23. Enceladus

Your energy anatomy has held you since before your birth. An intelligent organisation of elements, ether, air, fire, water and earth. Dynamic, yet stable, a simple dipole affords opportunity to mature your soul. To cradle a magnetic personality and in resonance exhaust your skill, through sustenance of a massive act of will. Life is a balancing act and you win the race when, in a state of ease, you choose to embrace your polarities. Positive, negative, objective, subjective, active, passive, alkaline, acid.

A-living for aeons, your resilient ions, simply and surely know what to do. If you can ensure that you favour neither side, then they will, for certain, help you gravitate toward what is true for you.

24. Contentment

All is love at inception. Susceptible to being intercepted by exceptional deception, the mind is then seized imperceptibly, lost in perception. Thoroughly taken and firmly yoked by, what is it, a creative engine or a cosmic joke? Suffering and pain will surely visit again and again. In turn, concepts refine by design, each time, unless, and until, receptive to contraception for this obdurate mind worm. The precept? Unfasten and accept, a concept-free[16] philosophy to identity. Life is not some perceived ideal, it is what it is. Listen, observe, get real. Relax, feel better return to love. Contentment is by

---

[16] JD Krishnamurti: "The description is not the described; I can describe the mountain, but the description is not the mountain, and if you are caught up in the description, as most people are, then you will never see the mountain."

far your best move. Believe me, to achieve certainty is easier than you can possibly conceive.

25. Gateway

Images from lore offer a little more in our quest, to recover the optimal state that is our rested-best. Like a double-edged sword parries and thrusts, our binary mind will compare and contrast to keep us fully engaged to the future and the past and to stay vulnerable to extremes and perpetually, shallow and manipulative memes. As Icarus teaches us through his misguided demise, don't be distracted by a mere conceptual prize. To live by it is to die by it, no matter how well it is wielded. Instead, listen passively to free yourself from this karmic bondage to remain safely shielded. To put your armour on, all you need do, is take it off. Through this embodiment you can safely execute your return from Oz, because, only through the act of love can you touch the night sky[17] above. Know that the I knows how, only you know when and there is no why! Where to start? Rely not on the I of the mind, but on the I of the heart. The former, the tree of knowledge, that sustains perceptual strife, the latter a gateway to happiness, the very tree of life. Habitual reliance on mere thinking must stop, if you are to become the divine ocean in this simply, human drop.[18] Before flowing out fully we have the key to enter in. Connected thus, the very universe is ours, as only when the sun sets can we see the stars. Sense it, feel it, trust it, love it and above all begin. In this super-position, no effort is required. Simply choose and feel inspired.

---

[17] Derived from "Only from the heart, can you touch the sky", a poem by Rūmī.

[18] "You are not a drop in the ocean, but the entire ocean in a drop" - Rūmī.

26. Crossing the Rubicon

There is very fine and a very distinct frontier that appears impermeable, when you have identified with concepts, created from a mindful perspective over your informative years. Although you may think that the die has been cast and the span of your life has been set, limits defined by the assumed scope of your mind suggests the extent to which the sweep of your awareness can plausibly aspire. No matter how hard you have tried to think yourself out of the box, the effort itself exhaustively expended, merely piles on more conceptual locks. To cross beyond the partition, constructed by your very own mindful volition, you need only accept that trying won't work and you can just choose to relax instead.

What opens then before you and within you,

will astound you, when you feel its simplicity and imperious reach. No need to pause as you step this way to reclaim the seat of your sovereign power, nor worry that you may pass a point of no return. Let go and be delightfully surprised in each and every conscious hour by what you can now learn.

27. Out of the Blue

Seemingly insulated. Stumbling, blindly muted. Bathed in fear. Constant, inconsistent effort ensures perpetual isolation. Seasoned observation clashes with concepts through experience. Healthy, practised imagination disappoints, despite impressive appearance. Thoughtful identification filters eternal fragrance, further frustrating understanding, through limited representation. Misguided, mindful attempts to storm the gates renders insight impossible, when all long the cosmic symphony[19] remains accessible, opening with ease to a deep and loving surrender, providing sanctuary to all, who give in. Trust

---

[19] The pioneers of plasma science (www.thunderbolts.info) inspired a new school of investigation called plasma cosmology. It has achieved surprising success in predicting major discoveries through observation.

instilled, certainty surprises, igniting inner ambition, flaming with co-creativity, seemingly at will. Obscuring clouds and illusory blue sky above, acquiesce, to a sea of stars where dark, teeming ocean tides stream toward love.

28. Sheltered Path

OK, before I go berserk, tell me, exactly[20] how does this relaxation gig work? Well, it's so simple that if you blink you will miss it, but it's not what you think. From a standing start, simply identify not with your head, but your heart. You will not begin to get this until you take a step toward it, and if that is what you want. This path will only start to show, when you dispense with what you think you know and dwell on someone, or something, you love instead. Kindle that feeling in your heart, touching nothing else, let the warmth from this lamp spread. The flame will grow and you will know more than the mind's filters can ever reveal. No content nor effort required, just love to relax, to be real.

---

[20] Rick Venning, thanks for the question I had not thought to ask.

29. Mindful Meditation

If love's feeling eludes you, do not be downcast. It's not the only way to still the mind and ignite your personal, pilot light. Simply and deeply now breathe, nice and slow. Take some time to settle and there you go. In and down. Up and out. In and down. Up and out. In and out. In and out. Focus your attention at the top of your chest, as the air flows past. In and down. Up and out. In and out. In and out. Imagine now as you settle, that this slow, empyreal current flows gently through a silken, gossamer-thin web, delicately seized as it progresses, momentarily arrested. The web flutters and fills, the passing air spills and you feel its delicate pull. In and down. Up and out. In and out. In and out. Slowly, in and out. As time passes by a warming sensation tenderly, perceptibly, sustains your attention.

This glow spreads and a relaxing feeling of warmth grows within your chest. Kindle that feeling, as best you can, touching nothing else. Let the warmth from this lamp spread. The flame will grow and through the feeling instilled, you will know more than the mind's filters can ever reveal. No content nor effort required, just love to relax, to be real.

30. Alignment

The mind is a very useful tool for sure, but it's not who you are, you are so much more. With attention re-balanced between your cardiac and nervous systems, you regain a quantum state, a super-position. Connected now, both outside and in, a flow is set up twixt the two and your intelligent energy starts to spin. The circumpunct, the circle and the dot, forms an ancient conjunction. A 2D representation of what happens now as you access so much raw information. In 3D and more the flow goes toroidal, a portal opens you to a further dimensional place. A gate, far beyond your ideas of time and space. For the avoidance of doubt, you can find this out for yourself, by going in. Then, when body-mind, spirit and soul are so aligned, like Pegasus himself, you will no longer be so temporally confined. When you can again think and feel in equal measure you will dwell at the threshold of a wondrous treasure.

Right now, consider that one genuine, heartfelt moment is worth a million thoughts. Accept this, and then repeat, until mind, body and soul are coincident, coherent, whole, replete and your return to innocence complete.

How many lives will it have taken to let go thus? Maybe, in due course, you will know, but for now you must drop the thought of more jam tomorrow and appreciate this healthy state that is devoid of such mechanical pain and sorrow.

31. Superman

At his core he is a man of steel. Here to help you to find what it is to be real. To uncover that invincible summer that lays dormant midst the mind's winter. Your fretful wanderings, at dead of night, reveal the time has come to kindle a new kind of light. In the heart of the darkness of your mere being lies a feeling, which when nurtured with care, will transform into a flaming temple of fire. If you don't aspire to start you simply won't find out. So, learn to relax and feel better. Don't hide from it, reside in it, where there is no doubt. It is certainly not what you might think, for therein lies your fear, your kryptonite. Let go, accept and let it burn and you will realise, you will be more than alright, and not a little surprised, as your soul takes flight.

32. Sacred Lover

There is a deep need to appreciate how to learn to let go, to loosen reliance on thinking and begin again to feel instead.

Yet, even when you have learned to habitually take as much notice of your heart as your head, external events, can even then, be so prolonged and intense that you may again descend into the clutches of an anxious mind, seemingly spent. Remember, as you are both magician and your very own physician, the unknown is your forever home. Know that you can recover. Find time to rest and explore. Listen to your own Music. Be your own sacred lover and you will discover still more.

33. Courage

Before hope is gone and the light goes out.
Switch off to switch on, be in no doubt.

34. Paradox

I am glad to have scratched this particular itch. Now I know that love and fear don't play on the same pitch. How do you feel about this? Do you think you will switch?

35. New Light

I feel my way in the dark, opening to a love, beyond sensation, that defines itself through the consequences[21] of my relaxation.

---

[21] Noetics: Philosopher William James (1902). Bringing a scientific lens to the study of subjective experience, and to ways that consciousness may influence the physical world.

36. Chocolate

Conscious as I am and at rest in certainty, as warming chocolate softens in a bain-marie, relaxation opens me to a contagious love that so delightfully infects my life. Its radiant heat dissolving my loss, anxiety and isolation.

37. Welcome

Oh, golden one, vital and bright, what can be done to shine this new light, such that it can be seen by everyone? Simply, attune, feel it in your heart. Soon, a nourishing flow will start. This flow will, with patience, become a flood. Spirit and soul, conscious and whole, warming our water and our blood. Bathe in this glow and you will know what this life is for. A blessing for sure. Kia Ora.

38. Faith

It is not absurd to believe, that the greater I feel it in my heart and the more certain of self I become, I will know and trust that we are one. If we all develop faith in this simple little rule,[22] we can all realise the perfect, pure potential of Zero, The Fool.[23]

---

[22] Stephen Wolfram's book A New Kind of Science explores a fundamental new way of modelling complex systems by following very simple rules. It challenges the dogmatic dominance of mathematics through an exploration of the concept of computational equivalence.

[23] In Tarot "The Fool" is the most powerful card in the pack, symbolising our pure potential for transformation.

Epilogue

On putting the finishing touches to the final draft of this work I was presented with three, unsolicited quotes:

"In the midst of winter, I found there was, within me, an invincible summer." – Albert Camus.

"The time has come to turn your heart into a temple of fire." – Rumi.

"As Far as We Can Discern, the Sole Purpose of Human Existence is to Kindle a Light in the Darkness of Mere Being." – CG Jung.

I am very happy to take this synchronous event as a validation of my independently acquired stance and have woven all three pieces into the poem "Superman". Thanks Albert, Jalāl ad-Dīn and Carl-Gustav, you are all very much appreciated.

References and Notes

1. One of the two NLP Magic questions. Espoused in *The Way of NLP* by Joseph O'Connor and Ian McDermott, published by Thorsons, 2001.

2. "Out beyond the ideas of right doing and wrong doing, there is a field. I will meet you there" – Rūmī.

3. The renowned "Flow Sequence" developed by Graham and Lyn Whiteman and as described in their book *Stress Less, More Success*, published by 10-10-10, 2015.

4. Inspired by the book *Life is Tremendous* by Charles "Tremendous" Jones, wherein "whatever you believe, act as if it is true" challenges each of us to wrestle with the nature of belief.

5. Here I relate to the monumental publication that is *A Course in Miracles*, by Helen Schucman, published in 1976. A year-long study of daily affirmations. A challenging and transformative read.

6. Doctor Randolph Stone, the founder of Polarity Therapy used this term "the growing edge" to define our journey to challenge and push back our boundary conditions. Set out in two volumes, *The Complete Collected Works* by CLCS Wellness Books, Dr Stone's system is a vast treatise on the ancient modality of Energy Medicine. See www.ukpta.org.uk.

7. The Hindu concept of jnana yoga, vichara (self-enquiry) as explored in David Godman's book *Be As You Are*, published by Penguin; reissue edition March 7, 1991.

8. Inspired by a conversation in an episode in series one of Star Trek Discovery, a Netflix Original Series, 2017.

9. Inspired by the book *Krishnamurti and the Unity of Man* by Carlo Suares, published in 1982 by Chetana, wherein Krishnamurti describes the moment when we become finally and fully disappointed by the mind.

10. The affectionate name for a horse-drawn carriage with a clear glass front. Also, a term used to define the heir apparent

within the British Monarchy. Here re-framed as the vehicle for radical reclamation of *our* sovereignty, a state in which we see the road ahead clearly, concurrent with experiencing the journey, safely and in comfort.

11. www.restedbest.co.uk

12. Trademark re-printed here with kind permission of www.heartenterprises.co.uk.

13. Central to "The Esencia Model" presented at www.esencia.org.uk and beautifully articulated in the song "Audition (The Fools Who Dream)", from the Original Motion Picture Soundtrack of La La Land 2016.

14. The Consequences of Relaxation as defined at www.lionhearted.org.uk

15. Poem of William Carlos Williams, American Poet, 1883-1963.

16. JD Krishnamurti: "The description is not the described; I can describe the mountain, but the description is not the mountain, and if you are caught up in the

description, as most people are, then you will never see the mountain."

17. Derived from "Only from the heart, can you touch the sky", a poem by Rūmī.

18. "You are not a drop in the ocean, but the entire ocean in a drop" – Rūmī.

19. The pioneers of plasma science (www.thunderbolts.info) inspired a new school of investigation called *plasma cosmology*. It has achieved surprising success in predicting major discoveries through observation.

20. Rick Venning, thanks for the question I had not thought to ask.

21. Noetics: Philosopher William James (1902). Bringing a scientific lens to the study of subjective experience, and to ways that consciousness may influence the physical world.

22. Stephen Wolfram's book *A New Kind of Science* explores a fundamental new way of modelling complex systems by following very simple rules. It challenges the dogmatic dominance of mathematics

through an exploration of the concept of computational equivalence.

23. In Tarot "The Fool" is the most powerful card in the pack, symbolising our pure potential for transformation.

ABOUT THE AUTHOR

Andrew Harry completed his therapeutic training as a Registered Polarity Therapy Practitioner (RPP) in Ireland in 2006, having qualified as an Advanced Practitioner in Neuro-Linguistic Programming (NLP) in London in 2005. He ran his own private practice in Bath UK for many years and has been a board member of the UK Polarity Therapy Association (UKPTA) since 2007.

Prior to his therapeutic career he served in the Royal Navy for 23 years, having graduated in Engineering in 1987 and obtaining his Royal Navy wings as a helicopter pilot. Prior to leaving military service, due to illness, he also qualified as a Chartered Management Accountant in 2004. He has worked since, both in his Private Practice in Polarity Therapy and in Local Government as a Service Accountant.

He lives with his wife Joy in Penzance, Cornwall, UK. He enjoys writing poetry and has a fine tenor voice. He continues to offer therapeutic services in Cornwall through his practise "Rested Best" and as a trainer of students at Esencia-Relaxation® under the auspices for The Relaxation Academy®.